Coloring book for adults and kids amazing corgi image for design

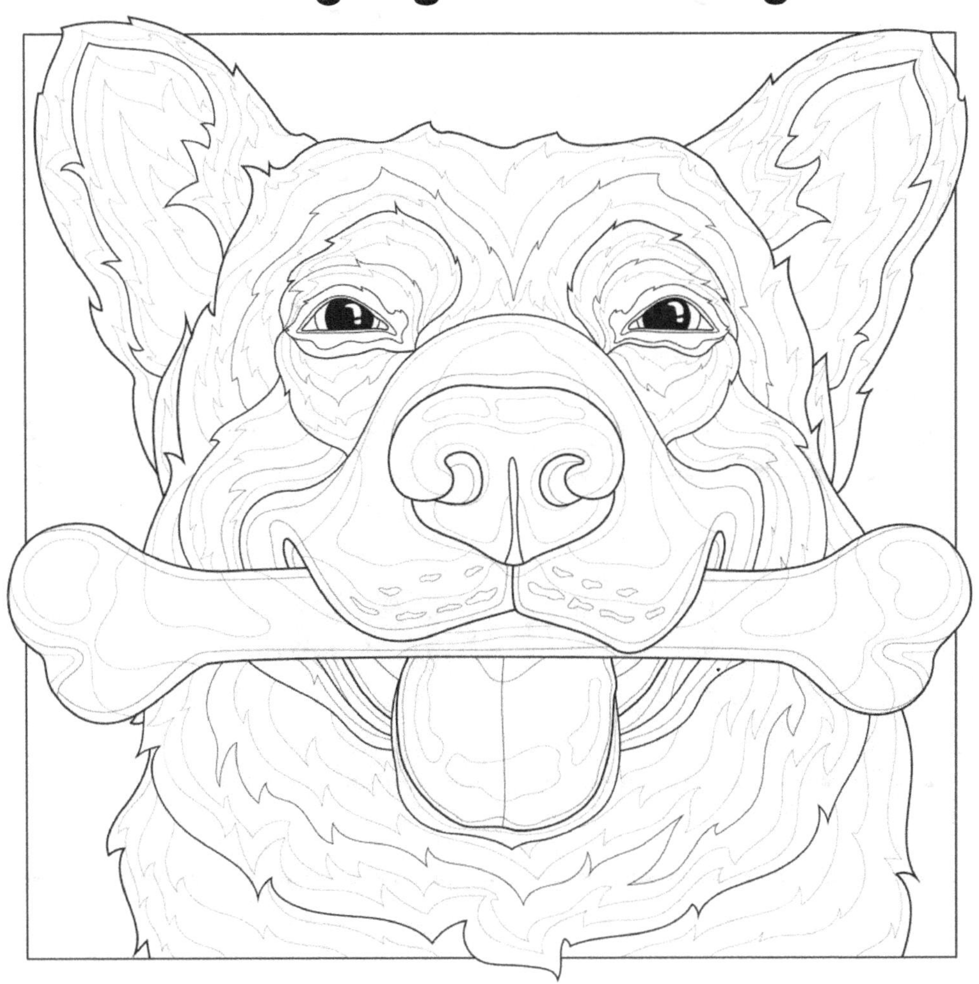

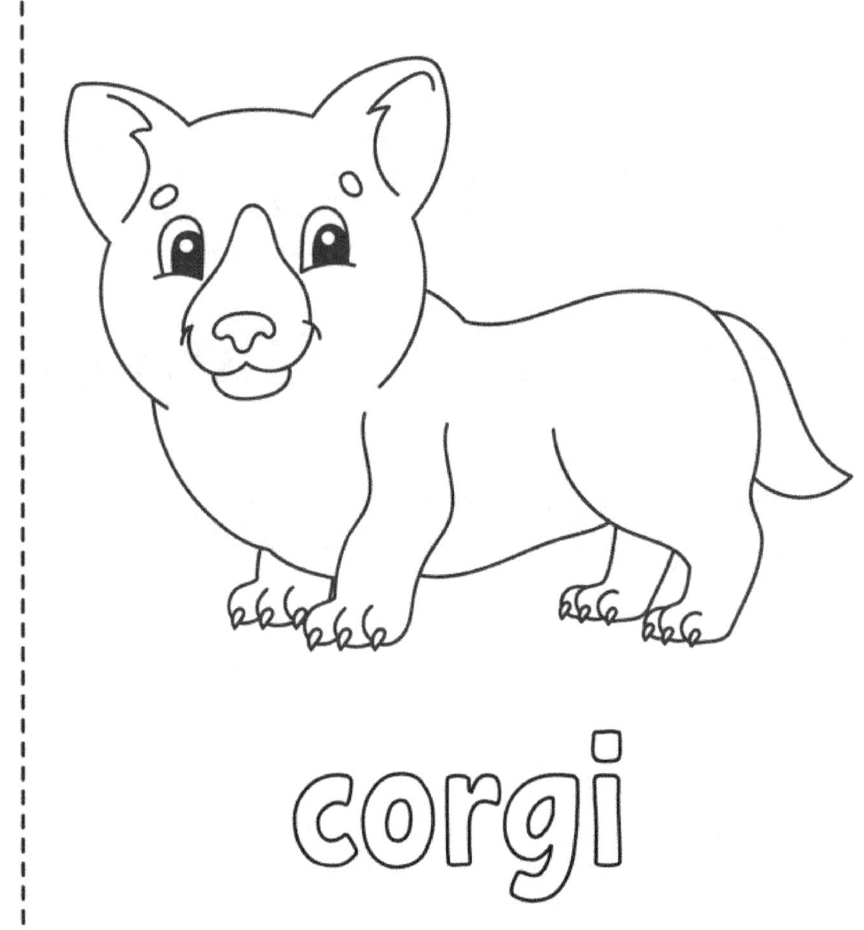

corgi

This coloring book is

belongs to

____

____

____

Cardigan Welsh Corgi

Cardigan Welsh Corgi

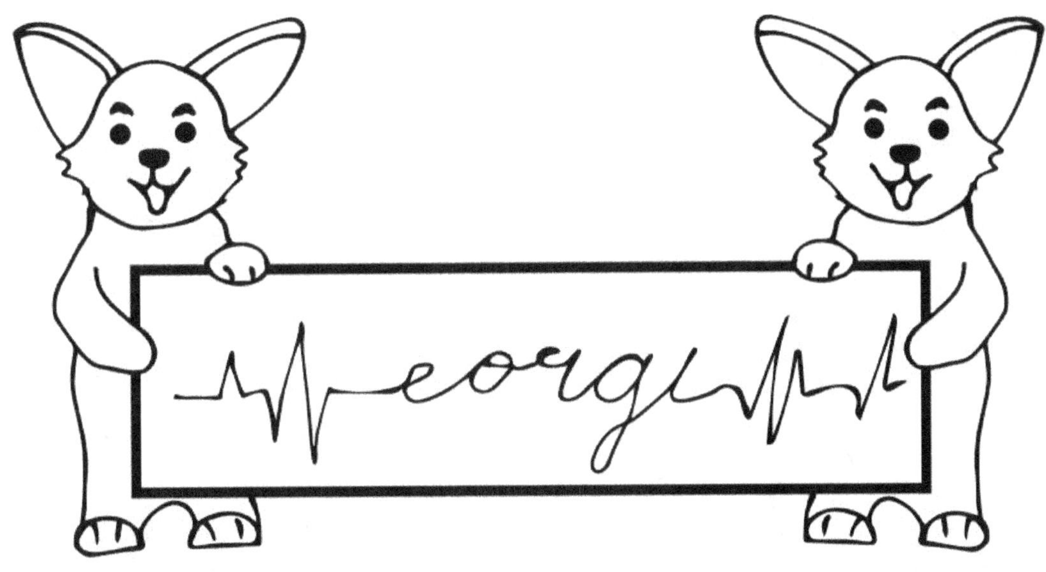

ABC game
for kids

corgi

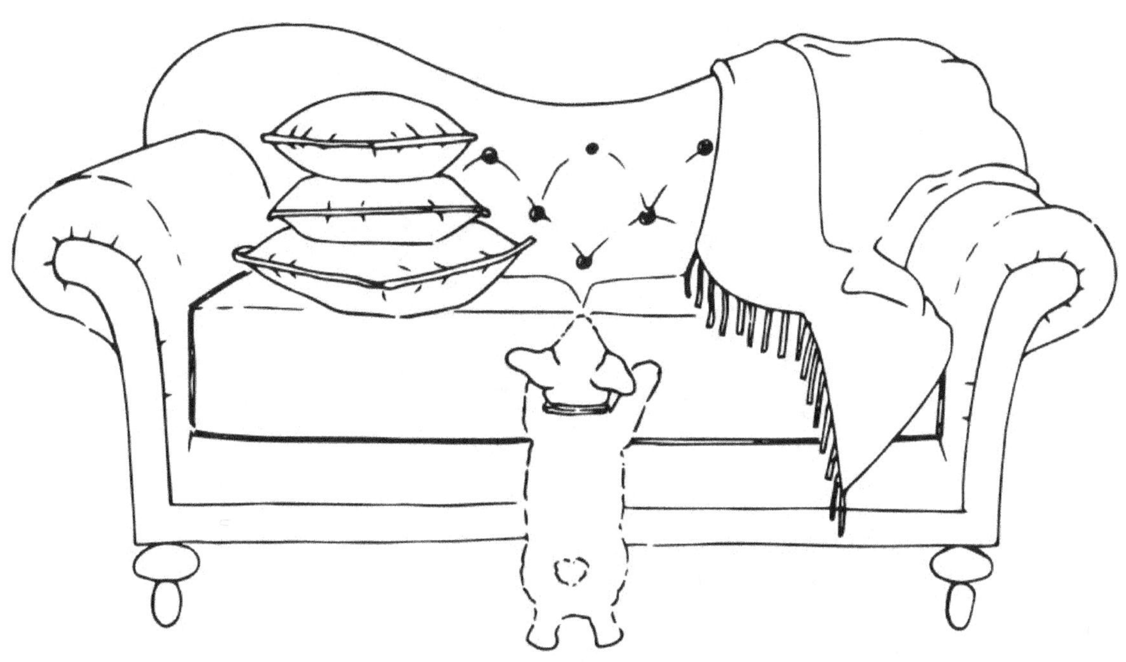

CORGI

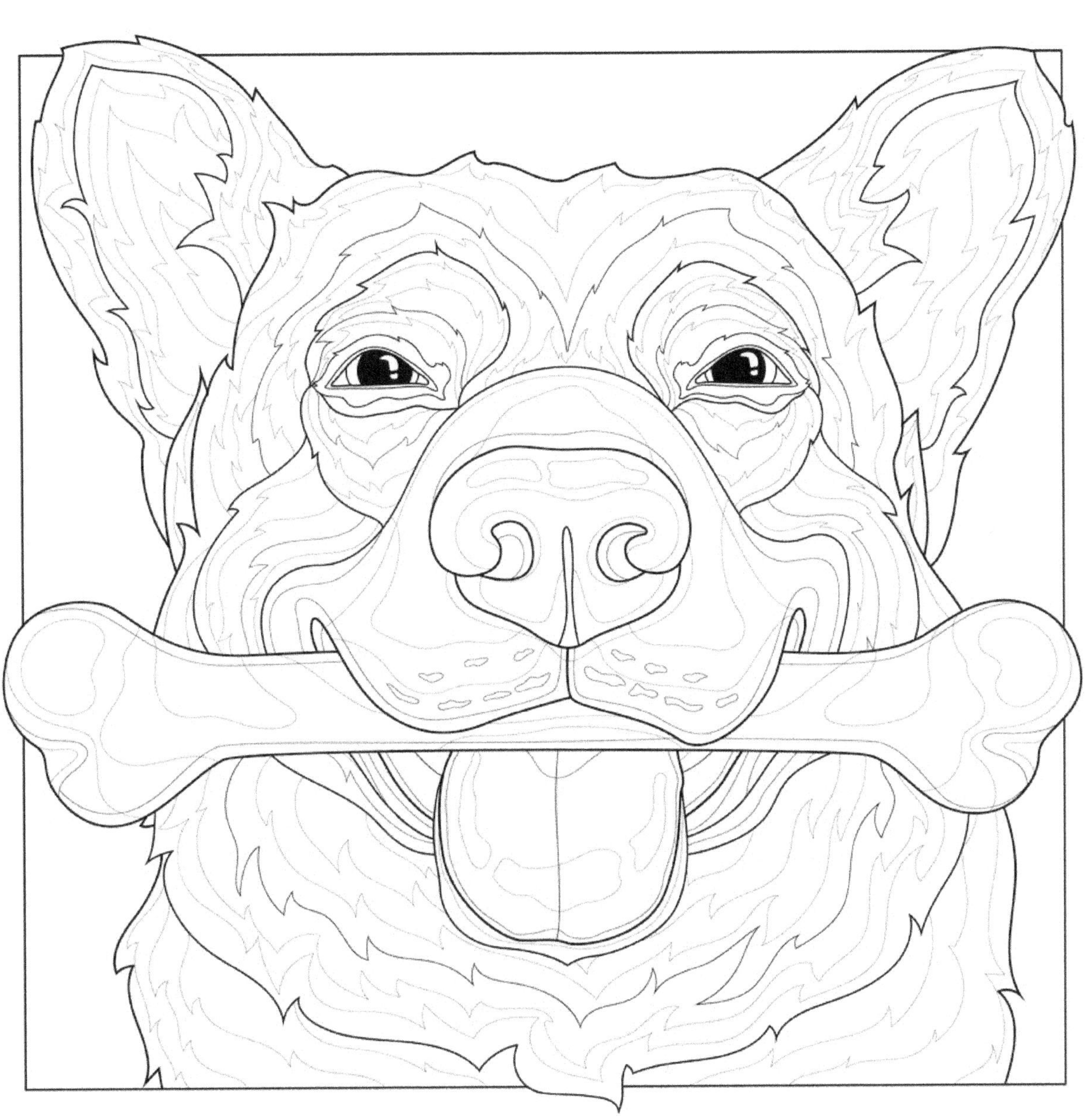

DOGS